THIS BOOK BELONGS TO:

_____

My Fashion Faves

My #1 favorite color: _____

My favorite item of clothing: _____

My favorite shoes: _____

My favorite accessories (jewelry, hair accessory, scarf, glasses):

_____

My favorite fashion person (it could be a fashion designer, a fashion model, an actress, or someone you know whose fashion sense you love):

_____

If I could create my own perfume, it would smell like...

_____

My color palettes

Make your own color combinations by coloring in these color palettes. You can repeat colors. Just be creative and have fun!

PALETTE #1
MY SIX FAVORITE COLORS

☐ ☐ ☐ ☐ ☐ ☐

PALETTE #2
SIX COLORS I LOVE WEARING

☐ ☐ ☐ ☐ ☐ ☐

PALETTE #3
COLORS THAT REMIND ME OF MY FAMILY

☐ ☐ ☐ ☐ ☐ ☐

PALETTE #4
COLORS THAT REMIND ME OF A HOT SUMMER DAY

PALETTE #5
COLORS THAT REMIND ME OF A COLD WINTER DAY

PALETTE #6
COLORS I THINK ARE ELEGANT

PALETTE #7
LOUD AND BRIGHT COLORS

PALETTE #8
SOFT AND CALM COLORS

Create lovely patterns on this wide brim hat.

Add some fun patterns to these boring looking socks.

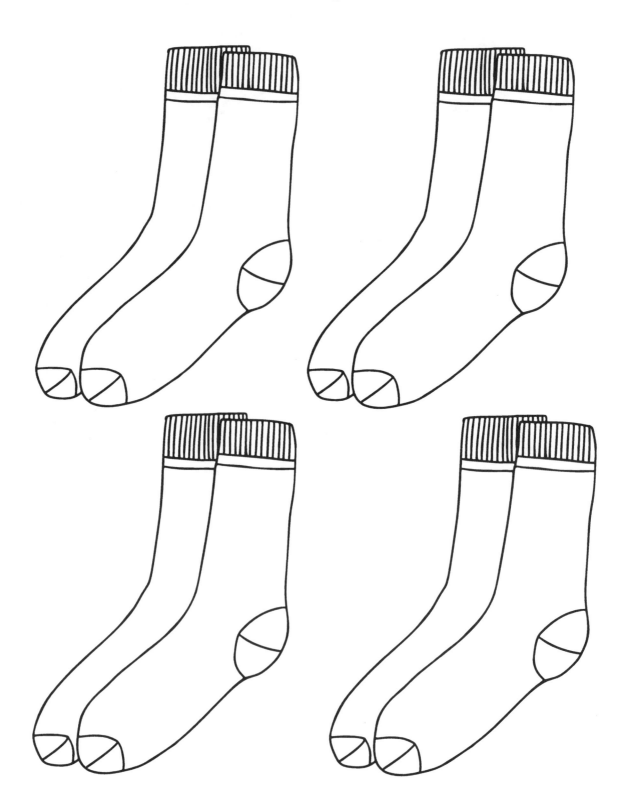

Make these ones more than fun...
Make them crazy!

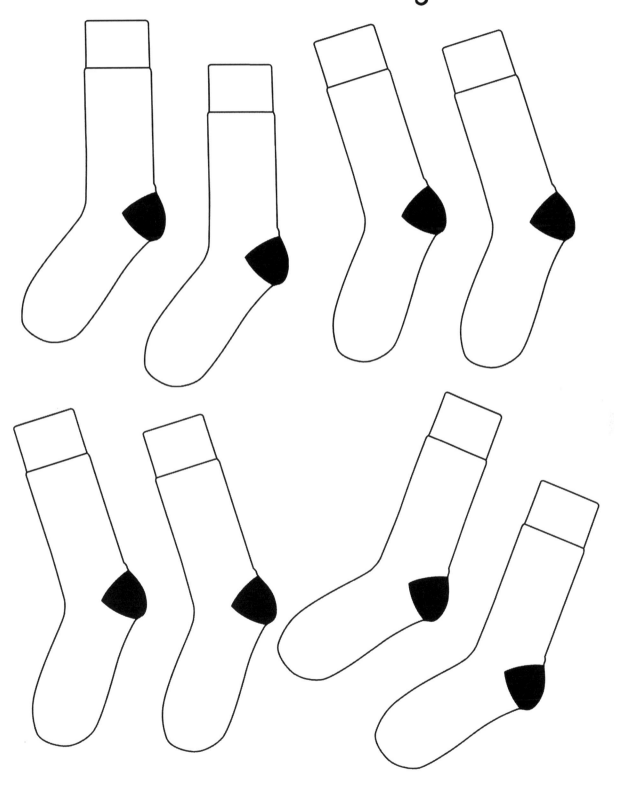

Design these platform heels for your favorite singer.

Who said loafers can't be stylish? Be creative and explore different color combinations.

Design these glasses thinking of your favorite colors.

Create designs that are perfect for the beach.

Give these flats unique looks that
you can't find in stores.

Design this handbag for a special occasion.

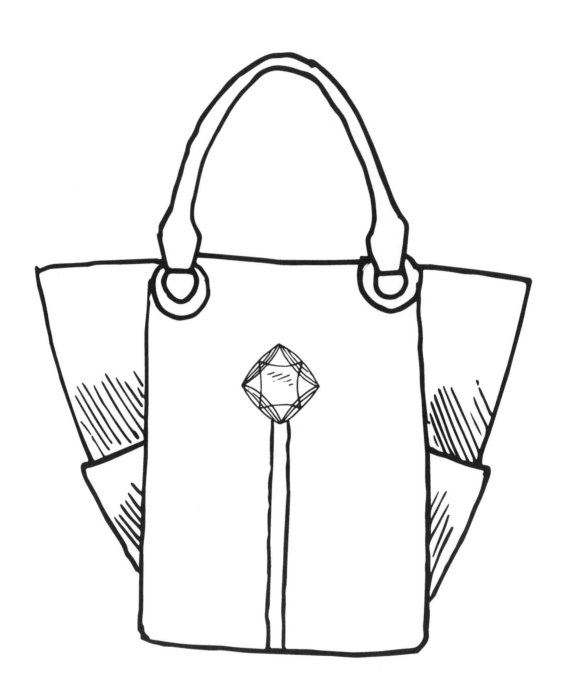

Design these bags for a fashionista who loves to travel.

Sofi is 6 years old. She loves unicorns and princesses. It is her first time travelling. Design a bag she can carry onto the plane.

Use different shades for each later of this dress.
Feel free to add sleeves too.

Some shoes have detailed decorations.
Carefully design these shoes as you explore
different shoe decorations.

Design two pairs of shoes for a girl who will be dancing all night.

Design a lovely travelling collection inspired by someone in your family.

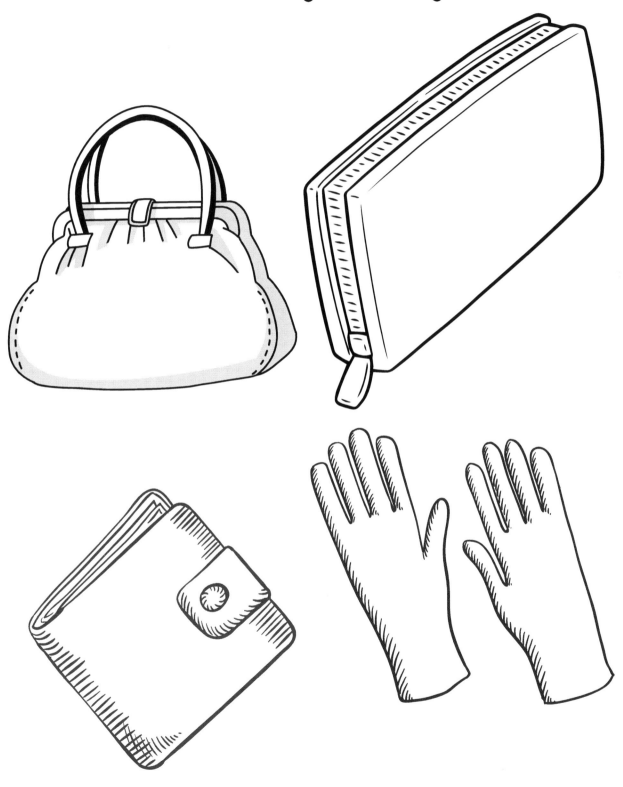

Anna Sui is a famous fashion designer who has also designed beautiful handheld mirrors, hair brushes, makeup brushes, and more. Anna Sui uses a lot of flowers and butterflies in her designs.

Design your own collection of beauty items with your unique sense of style.

Design challenge: Design a baby clothes collection and give the collection a cute name.

Get inspired by Autumn colors to design this shoe collection.

*Think of the color of your favorite warm beverage/drink (tea, latte, hot chocolate)

Design these bows WITHOUT using pink. You can do it!

Diana is going to her best friend's wedding. Create an elegant makeup look for her.

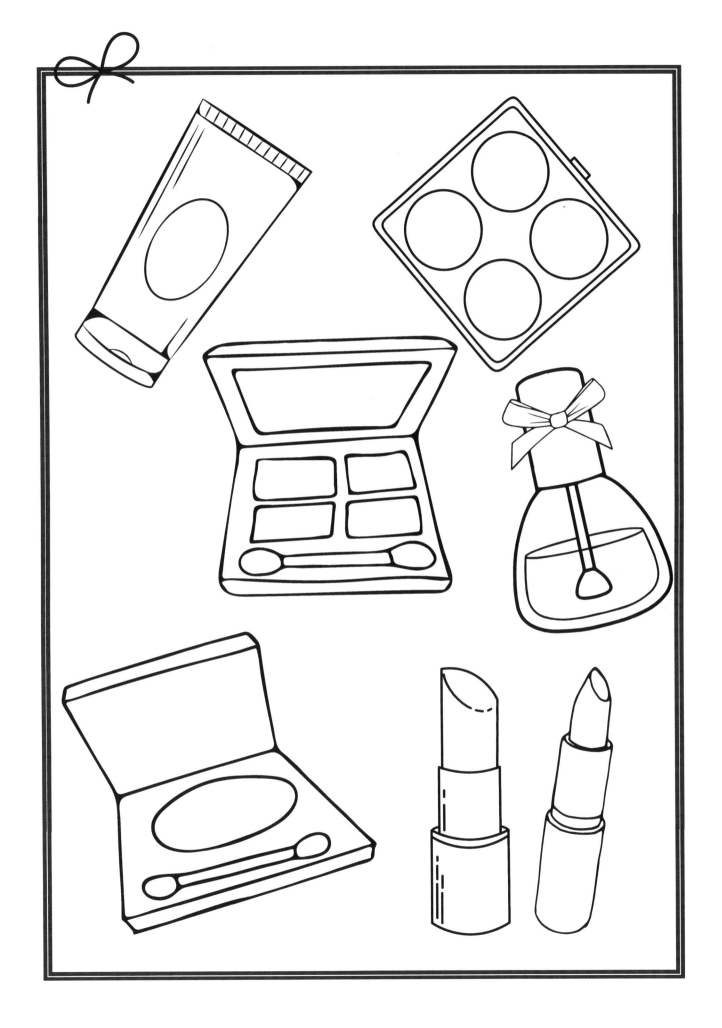

Design these perfume bottles inspired by your favorite scents. Give each bottle a name.

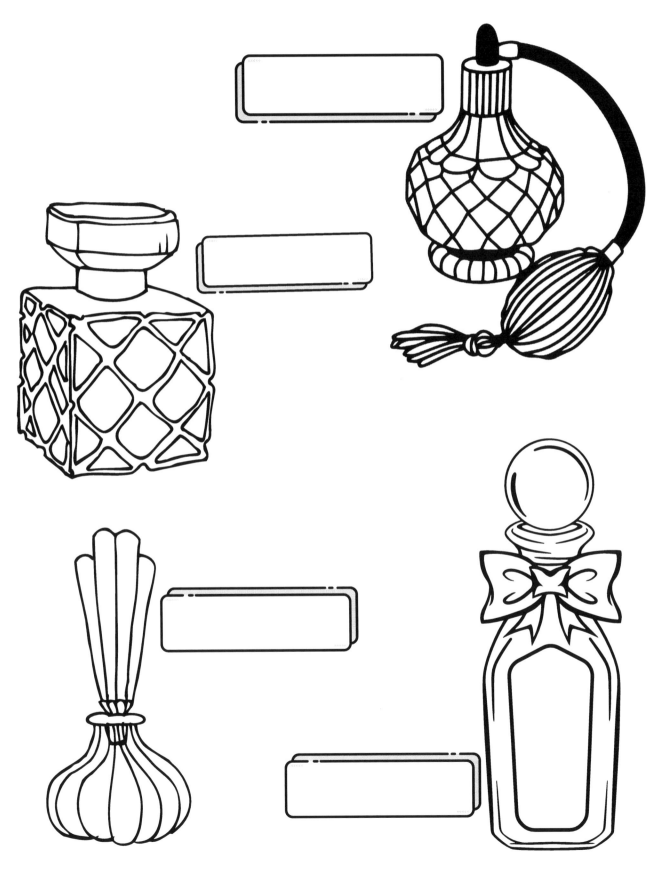

Decorate this blouse with cool geometric shapes.

Design a colorful flip flop collection.

Design a coat you would gift your mom.

Design a warm winter collection.

Make this dress extra elegant by adding some stripes.

Cousins Mia and Tina are going shopping. They want to be comfortable but also look fashionable.

Design a pair of shoes to match this dress.

→

Make these heels extra classy!

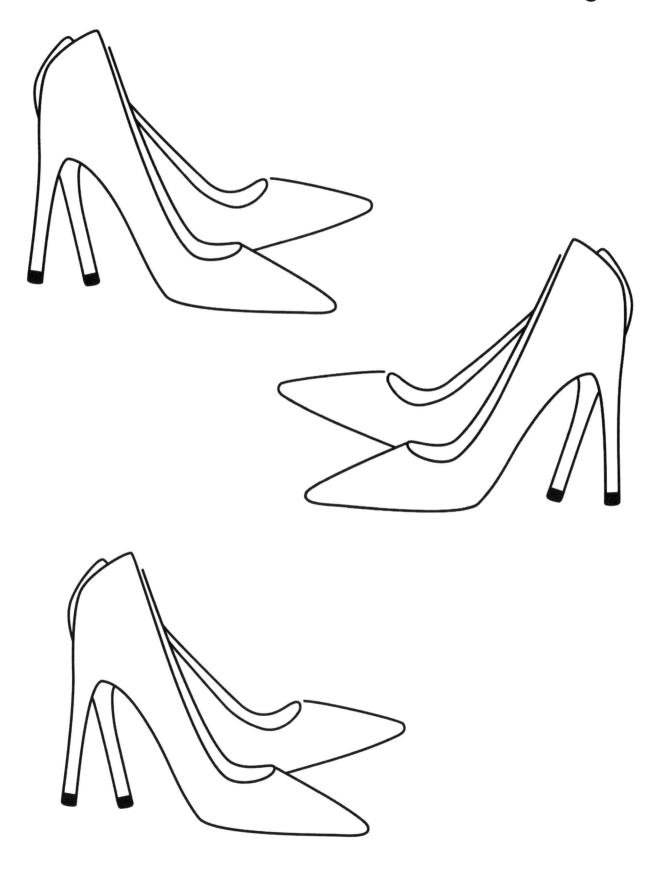

These shoes need some sparkly jewelry.

Design a unique school backpack. Feel
free to add more pockets and zippers.

Design an outfit that is warm and comfy to wear when studying at the library.

Create a sweatpants collection for your country's Olympics team.

Design a hoodie both girls and boys can wear.

How do you feel on rainy days? Express that feeling as you design this rainy day collection.

Design some matching raincoats for a family of three (mother, father and child)

Challenge: Turn these sneakers into a work of art. Get inspired by paintings you have seen on walls and in museums.

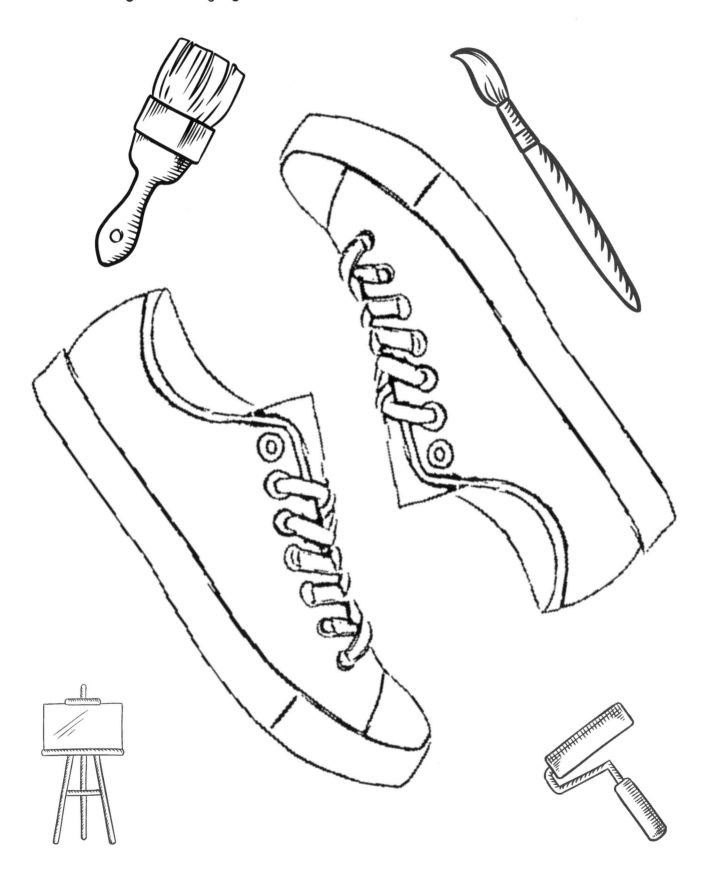

Use flowers to design a matching sneaker/bag collection.

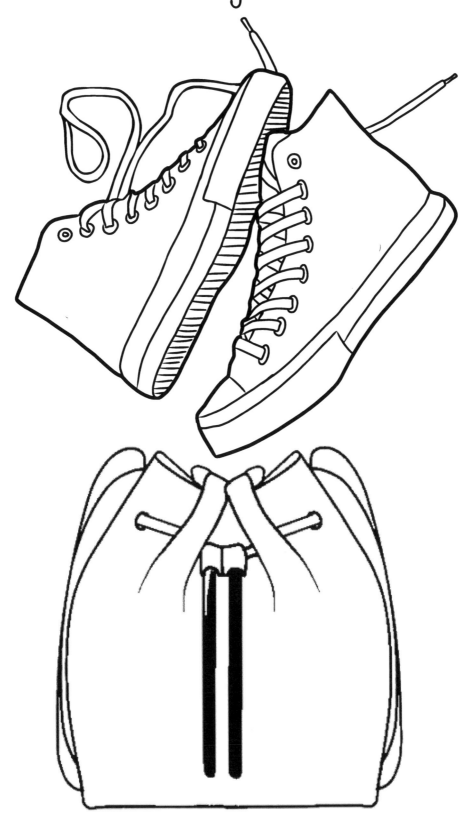

Use colors that remind you of
ice cream, beach sand and tropical fruits as you design.

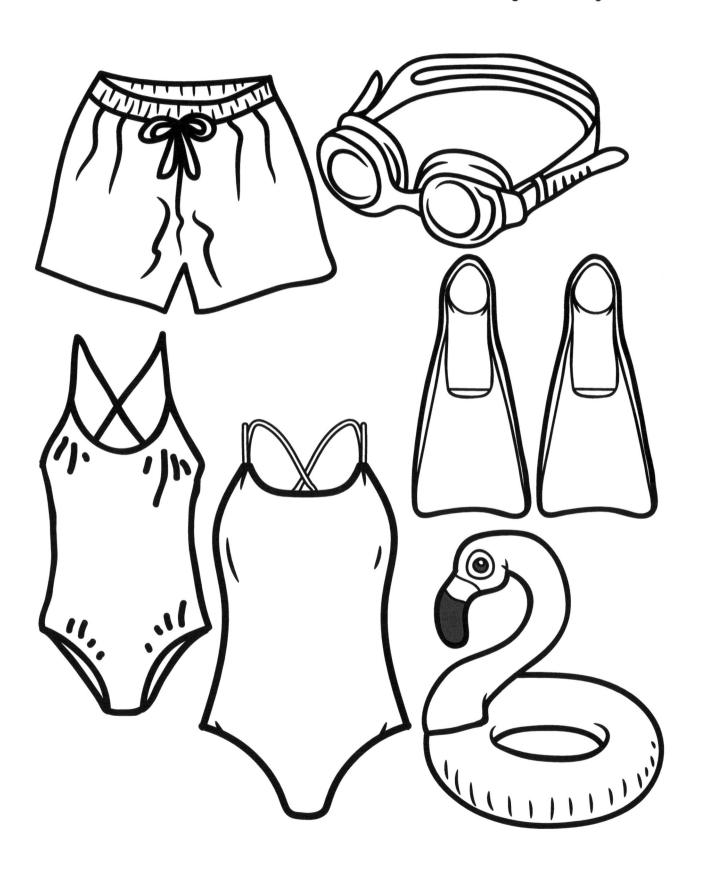

Write your favorite word on this T-shirt
and decorate it.

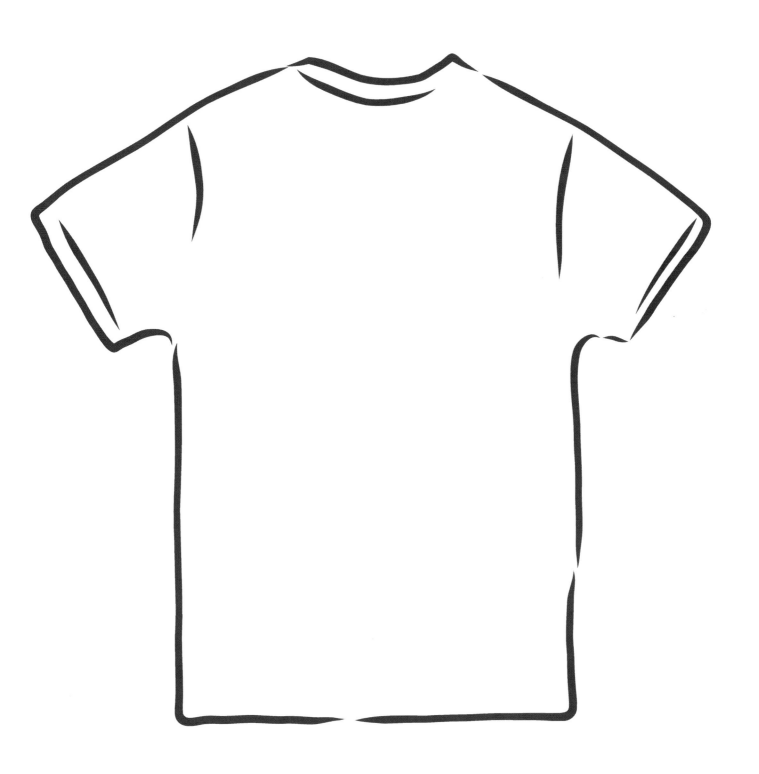

Design 2 cheerleading uniform options for your local cheerleading team.

Design hair accessories for your cheerleaders to wear.

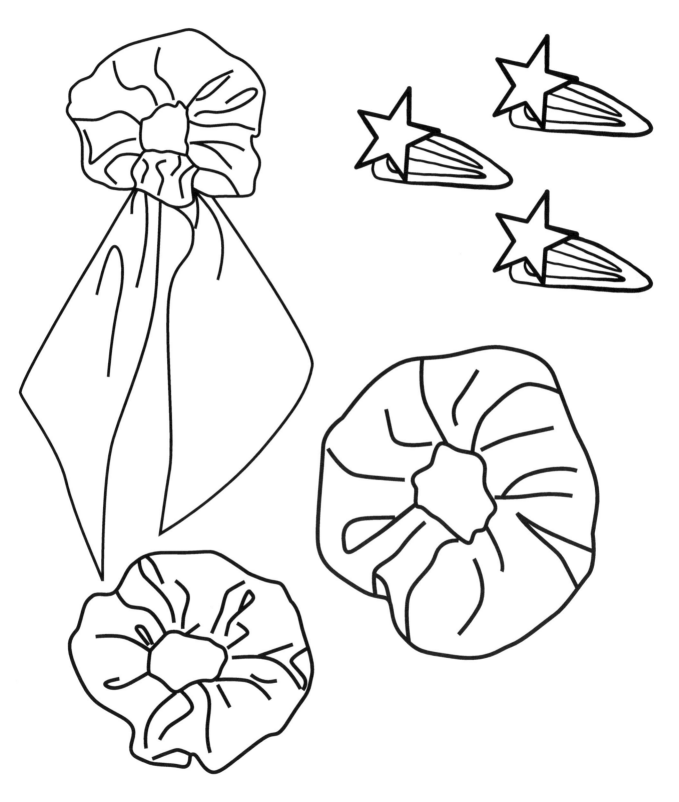

Decorate this bomber jacket for someone who loves nature.

Here are some badges to help you get inspired.

Turn this into an elegant night robe for a modern day princess.

Design some beaded jewelry to share with your best friends.

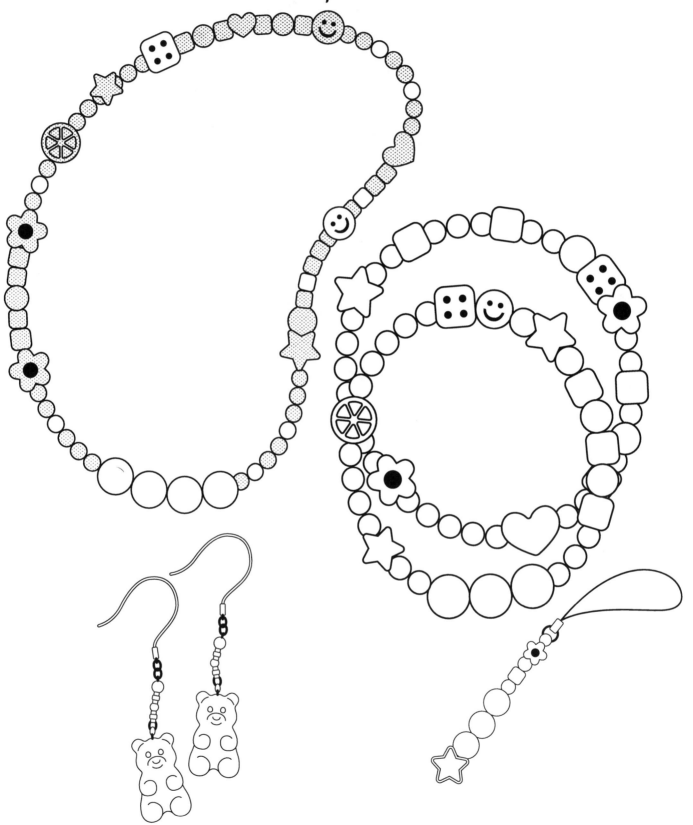

Get inspired with these patterns!

Houndstooth

Polkadot

Gingham

Herringbone

Animal Print

Paisley

Create a skirt that matches each blouse.

Imagine when and where you would wear each of these skirts, then design.

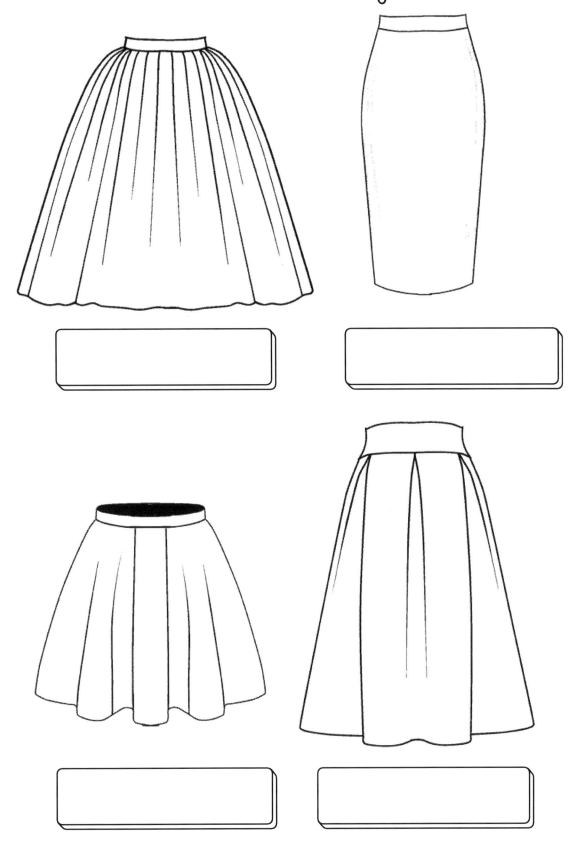

You have been hired to design the coolest waterproof watches for scuba divers. Get inspired by the colors of the beach and sea life as you design.

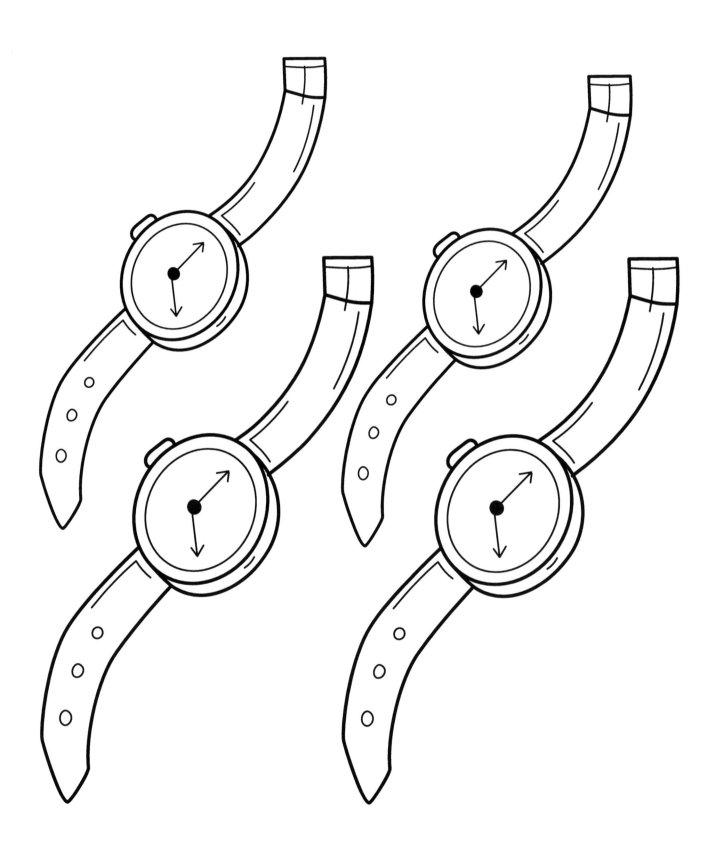

Design a trendy sweater that matches this black skirt.

Challenge: Draw or write something funny on these t-shirts.

Design these vests into something cool you would want to wear.

Design an office outfit.

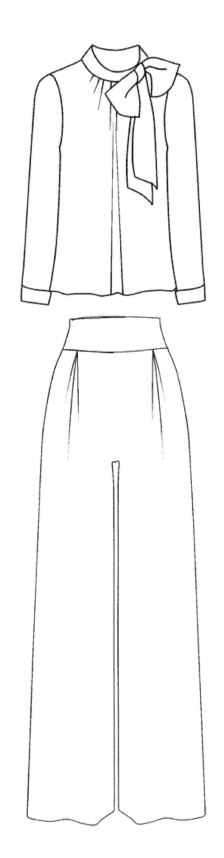

Color in these nail polishes with all your favorite colors?

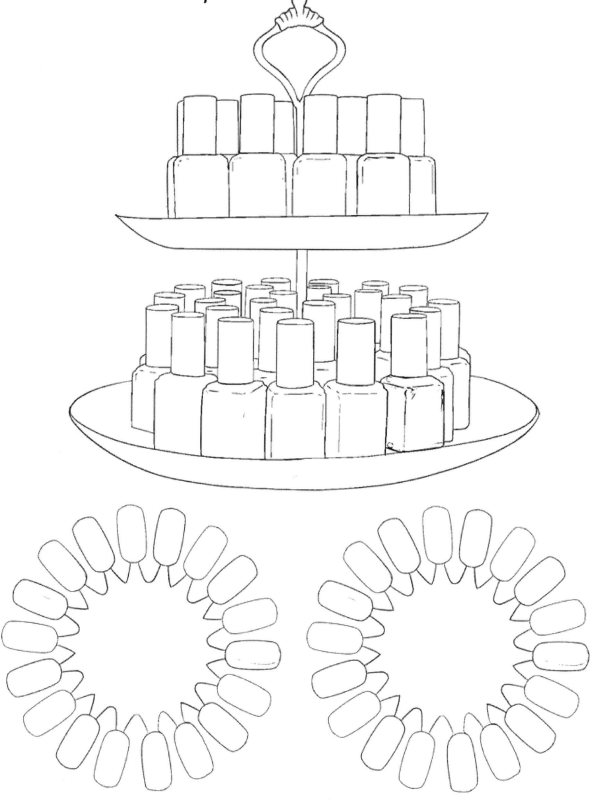

Have fun with some nail art!

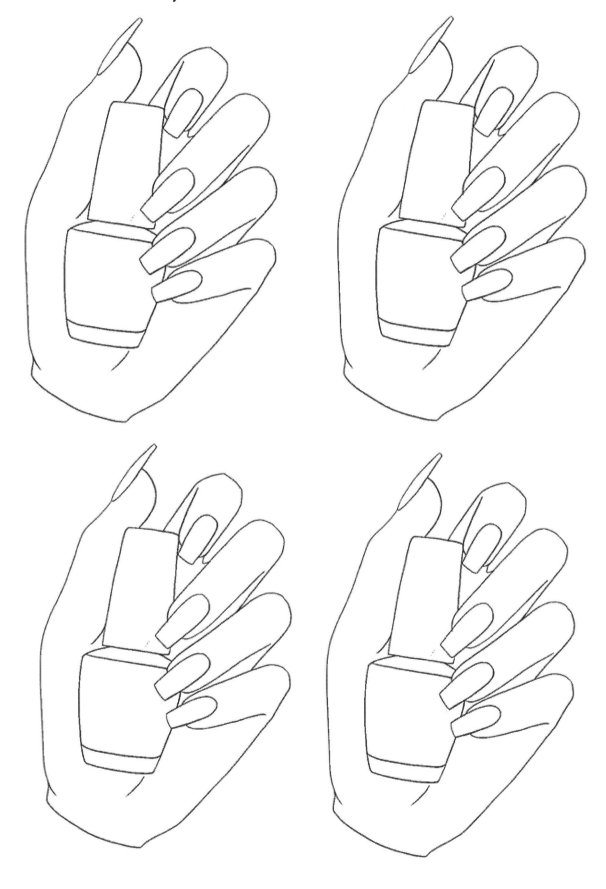

Create a logo for this t-shirt. It's for some who loves sports.

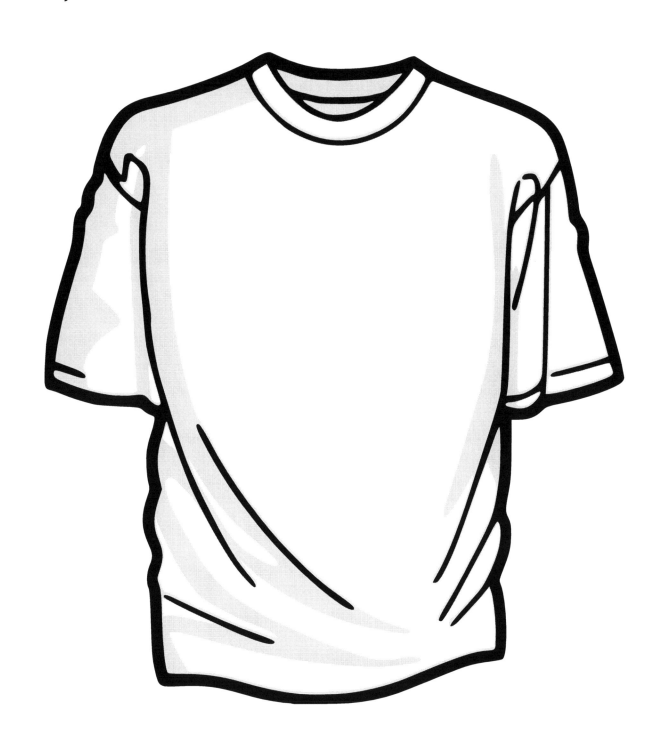

Design a tote bag with a message to save the planet.

Please make this the ugliest Christmas sweater ever!

Design some beautiful Aloha shirts.

Fun fact: Aloha shirts are also known as Hawaiian shirts.

Add some beautiful hairclips.

Design a fashionable collection for a yogi.

Design something comfortable you would wear at home.

Design a fashionable makeup bag.

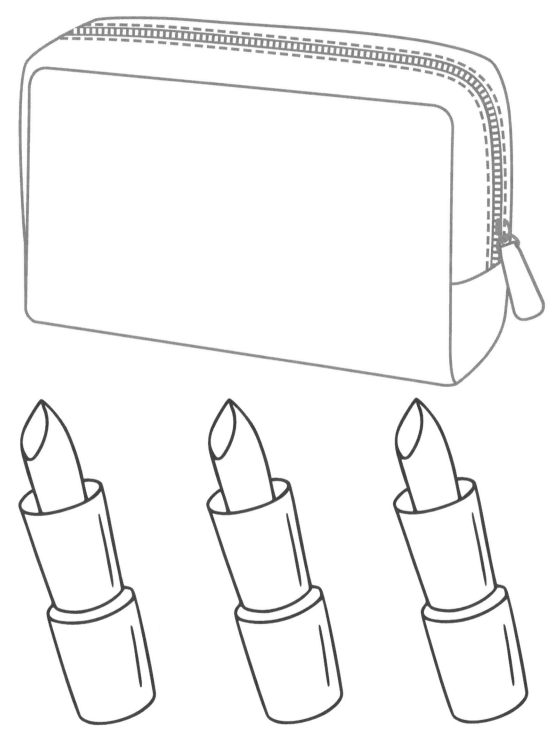

What are your favorite lipstick shades?

Susan needs your help picking some nail polish colors.
Make a few color suggestions and create some nail art combining all these colors.

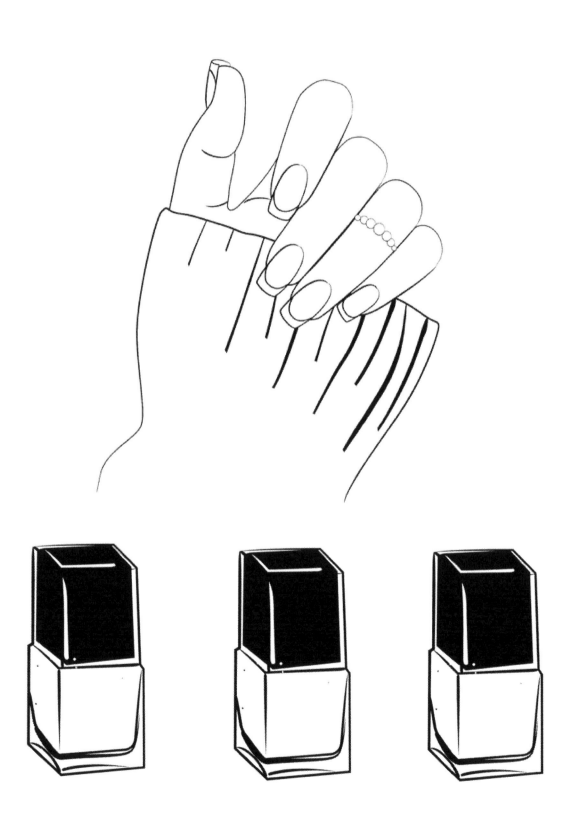

Challenge: Design theses super comfy sandals for a Summer fashion show!

Challenge: Add things to make this sweater and gloves more fashionable. Use your imagination!

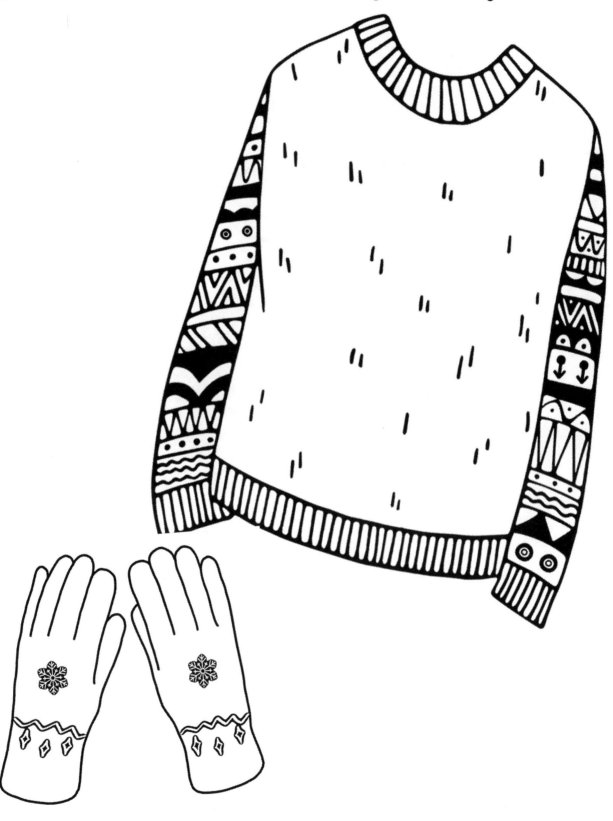

Design these paisley-patterned pants for a fashion show.

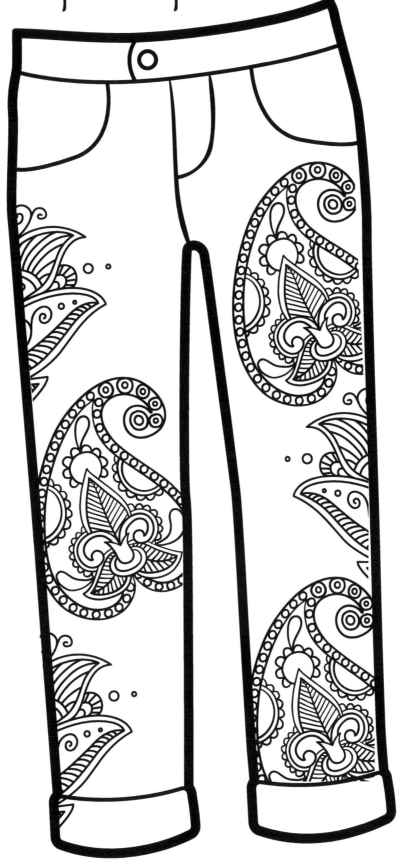

Have fun being a jewelry designer for a day!

Can you fill this page with amazing jewelry that you would store in these precious jewelry boxes?

Design mismatching jeans for you and your best friend.

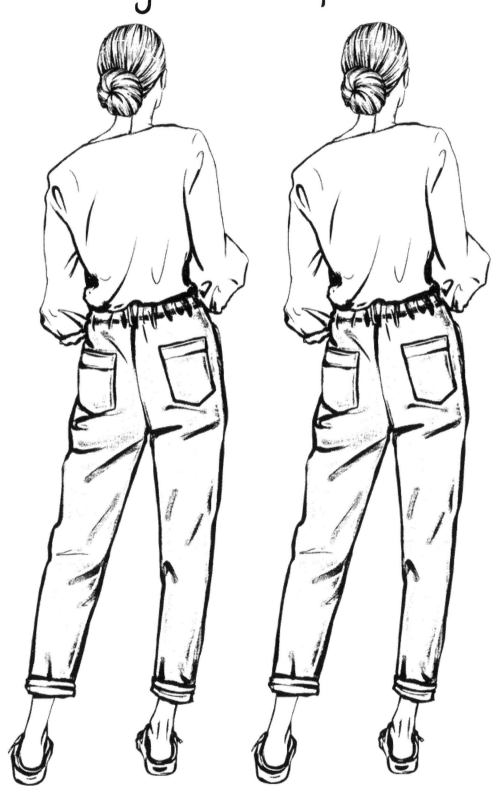

Make a design choice:
Bright fluorescent colors or bold elegance?

Make a design choice:
For a family dinner or for a day at the office?

Design 3 bridesmaid dresses.

Draw an amazingly beautiful wedding dress.

How did you like this book?

I am a small independent publisher who loves creating
books like the one you are holding.
Thank you so much for giving this book a home!
I put a lot of love and thought into making it. I hope you
enjoyed using this book as much as i enjoyed making it.

If you would like to leave a review for this book on Amazon

or

if you would like to find more books like this,
scan the QR code below to visit my author central page.

Thanks!

Mariel

SCAN ME

Made in the USA
Monee, IL
14 February 2023

27776703R00066